Top Tips and Practice
for PTE Young Learners

QUICKMARCH & BREAKTHROUGH

T0345691

Contents

Introduction

Hello!

This book will help you to prepare for the PTE Young Learners *Quickmarch* and *Breakthrough* tests.

The first part of this book will help you prepare for the tests, and includes:

* useful grammar tips, topics and words for *Quickmarch* and *Breakthrough*
* general exam tips
* irregular verb lists
* regular verb tips
* activities and tips in the *Strategies and Exercises* section
* self-assessments for each test in the *Strategies and Exercises* section.

The second part of the book has two past papers for you to complete, one for *Quickmarch* and one for *Breakthrough*. Try to complete each paper in one attempt. If you get a good score, you'll be ready for the actual test!

The *Quickmarch* written test is divided into six tasks:

* Task One tests your listening skills
* Task Two tests your listening and writing skills
* Tasks Three and Four test your reading and writing skills
* Tasks Five and Six test your writing skills.

The *Quickmarch* spoken test is divided into two tasks:

* Task One has a question and answer based on a board game
* Task Two has short talks based on topic cards, such as *my last school trip*, *last weekend* and *my last birthday*.

The *Breakthrough* written test is divided into six tasks:

* Task One and Two test your listening skills
* Tasks Three and Four test your reading and writing skills
* Tasks Five and Six test your writing skills.

The *Breakthrough* spoken test is divided into two tasks:

* Task One has a question and answer based on a board game.
* Task Two is a short talk, and question and answers based on topic cards, such as *a bad day for me* and *my family*, *a great day* and *transport in my town or city*.

The audio scripts and answer keys for this book can be found online.

General exam tips

Before the test

- Review the test structure.
- Look back through your English notebook and review the important things
- Check the word list in your book (see pages 8 and 9): do you remember all the words?
- Review the grammar points in your book (see pages 8 and 9).
- Be ready with pencils, a sharpener, an eraser and your ID document.
- Go to the bathroom!

During the test

- Listen carefully to the examiner.
- Read the instructions on the test paper.
- If you do not understand what you have to do, raise your hand.
- Write the answers clearly.
- Check the answers: you can always erase and rewrite!
- Do not talk to others.

After the test

- Submit your test paper (first, check that you have written your name!).
- Collect all your things.
- Leave the classroom silently.
- Relax!
- Your test results will arrive by mail.

Good luck!

Irregular verbs

Here is the list of the main irregular verbs, with the *past simple* and *past participle*.

Remember! We use the *past participle* with the *present perfect* to talk about past events that are connected with the present. The *past simple* is used to talk about actions that have taken place and ended in the past.

Infinitive	Past simple	Past participle
become	became	become
begin	began	begun
break	broke	broken
bring	brought	brought
build	built	built
buy	bought	bought
catch	caught	caught
choose	chose	chosen
come	came	come
cost	cost	cost
cut	cut	cut
do	did	done
draw	drew	drawn
drink	drank	drunk
drive	drove	driven
eat	ate	eaten
fall	fell	fallen
feed	fed	fed
feel	felt	felt
fight	fought	fought
find	found	found
fly	flew	flown
forget	forgot	forgotten
forgive	forgave	forgiven
get	got	got
give	gave	given

Infinitive	Past simple	Past participle
go	went	gone
grow	grew	grown
have	had	had
hear	heard	heard
hide	hid	hidden
hit	hit	hit
hold	held	held
know	knew	known
learn	learnt / learned	learnt / learned
leave	left	left
lend	lent	lent
lose	lost	lost
make	made	made
mean	meant	meant
meet	met	met
pay	paid	paid
put	put	put
read	read	read
ride	rode	ridden
rise	rose	risen
run	ran	run
say	said	said
see	saw	seen
sell	sold	sold
send	sent	sent
set	set	set

Infinitive	Past simple	Past participle
show	showed	shown
sing	sang	sung
sit	sat	sat
sleep	slept	slept
speak	spoke	spoken
spend	spent	spent
stand	stood	stood
steal	stole	stolen
swim	swam	swum

Infinitive	Past simple	Past participle
take	took	taken
teach	taught	taught
tell	told	told
think	thought	thought
throw	threw	thrown
understand	understood	understood
wear	wore	worn
win	won	won
write	wrote	written

Regular verbs

For all **regular verbs**, the past tense is formed by adding the suffix -**ed**.

Remember! Regular verbs follow some **spelling rules** for adding the suffix -**ed**.

- If the verb ends with e, only -d is added:
  chase → chased
- If the verb ends with a vowel + y, add -ed:
  stay → stayed
- If the verb ends with a consonant + y, we substitute the y with an i and add -ed:
  study → studied
- If the verb ends with a stressed vowel and a consonant, double the final consonant and add -ed:
  stop → stopped
- If the verb ends with the letter l, double the l and add -ed:
  travel → travelled

For the *Quickmarch* test, you need to know ...

... these grammar points:

- **The verb 'to be' in the past simple tense**
  was, were
- **The past simple tense**
  walked / I didn't walk / Did you walk?
- **Irregular past forms of common verbs**
  went, got up, ate, drank, slept, came, ...
- **'Going to' to express future plans and intentions**
  I am going to visit my aunt next week. / I am going to work hard this year.
- **The present continuous to talk about the future**
  She's going out tonight.
- **'Can' for permission**
  Can we go to the cinema?
- **Comparatives of adjectives**
  Ben is older than Sophie. / Ben is better at English than Sophie.
- **Superlatives of adjectives**
  Anna is the youngest girl in her class.
- **Conjunction 'because'**
  Billy was late for school because he missed the bus.

... these topics:

- Spare time
- Places
- Jobs
- Illness
- Clothes
- Food
- Families
- Pets and animals
- School
- The body and people's appearance
- Toys
- Houses

... and these words:

- **Common spare time activities**
  swimming, dancing, playing computer games, ...
- **Hobbies**
  collecting stamps, solving puzzles, ...
- **Common jobs and professions**
  teacher, doctor, police officer, taxi driver, nurse, ...
- **Common illnesses**
  headache, toothache, sore throat, ...
- **Names of countries and nationalities**
  France, French, China, Chinese, Canada, Canadian, ...
- **Points of the compass**
  North, South, East, West
- **Basic geographical features**
  river, mountain, sea, lake, ...
- **Town facilities**
  museum, cinema, supermarket, library, ...
- **Shops and essential shopping items**
  baker's, bread, chemist's, medicine, newsagent's, newspaper, ...

For the *Breakthrough* test, you need to know …

… these grammar points:

- **The present perfect**
  Have you ever been to London? / I have never been to New York.
- **'Will' in all basic uses**
  We think Ben's team will win.
- **The first conditional with 'if'**
  If Annie finishes her homework, she will go out.
- **'Would' for polite offers**
  Would you like a cup of tea?
- **'Would (rather)' for preferences**
  I would rather go to the concert. / I wouldn't like to go to the football match.
- **The past continuous in narratives**
  Mr Brown was having breakfast when the phone rang.
- **The infinitive to indicate purpose**
  Grandmother made a cake to give to Diana.
- **Tag questions**
  She is, isn't she? / They will, won't they?

… these topics:

- The senses
- Nature
- Space and space travel
- Travel
- Jobs and professions
- Spare time
- Places
- Jobs
- Illness
- Clothes
- Food
- Families
- Pets and animals
- School
- The body and people's appearance
- Toys
- Houses

… and these words:

- **Words of senses and perception**
  smell, taste, look, sound, feel, sweet, beautiful, loud, rough, smooth, soft, sharp, heavy, …
- **Extinct and endangered wildlife**
  panda, snow leopard, whale, black rhino, dinosaur, …
- **Professions and jobs**
  teacher, doctor, dentist, hairdresser
- **Words connected with travelling**
  ticket, airport, delay, suitcase, …
- **Types of music**
  pop, rap, soul, rock, reggae, techno, …
- **Musical instruments**
  guitar, piano, keyboards, drums, …

Remember: for the *Breakthrough* exam, you also need to know the grammar, topics and words required for the *Quickmarch* exam.

Activities for *Quickmarch* Task 1

The *Listening* exercises can be difficult. Ask your teacher or parent to help you.

Remember:
- Read the instructions carefully.
- Listen to the audio twice.
- Listen for information you need to complete the exercise.
- Only one picture is correct.
- Check your answers.

TOP TIPS

First, look at the pictures.
- What do you see in the pictures?
- Who do you see?
- How do they look?
- What are they doing?
- What other information is in the picture (time, date, …)?

Do Exercises 1, 2 and 3 on page 11.

Do you need to review the grammar?

Review
- *going to*
- the *present continuous* to talk about the future
- the *past simple* of regular verbs.

Think about these topics:
- *months of the year*
- *weather*
- *wild animals.*

☞ In Exercise 1, choose the correct picture (A or B).

In **recording** 🎧2 (page 44), you will hear six important details.

Remember: you have to listen for specific information.
- Circle the positive information you hear in the audio (for example: *I want to go and see the kangaroos.*).
- Cross out the negative information in the audio (for example, *America? No way!*).

☞ In Exercise 2, choose the correct picture (A or B).

In **recording** 🎧3 (page 44), you will hear the information you need.

Remember: only one picture is correct.

☞ In Exercise 3, choose the correct picture (A, B or C).

In **recording** 🎧4 (page 44), you will hear the information you need.

Remember: listen for the keywords (see the highlighted words on page 44).

1. Listen to recording 🎧2 and look at the pictures. Where does Nick want to go? Put a cross under picture A or B.

2. Listen to recording 🎧3 and look at the pictures. Read the questions and put a cross under picture A or B.

1. When does Olivia want to go and visit Tom?

2. How long did Tom visit them for?

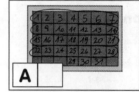 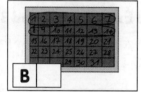

3. When do they decide to go?

3. Listen to recording 🎧4 and look at the pictures. Read the questions and put a cross under picture A, B or C.

1. Where does Nick want to go for the winter holidays?

2. Where are the Green family going for their winter holidays?

3. Where did they go for their winter holidays last year?

Activities for *Quickmarch* Task 2

The *Listening* exercises can be difficult. Ask your teacher or parent to help you.

Remember:

- Read the instructions carefully.
- Listen to the audio twice.
- Listen for information you need to complete the exercise.
- The conversation is in parts.
- Only write short answers.
- Check your answers.

TOP TIPS

First, read the questions.

- Are the questions about *who* or *what*?
- What information should you listen for a time (place or a name)?
- Do you need information about the past, the present or the future?

Do Exercises 1, 2 and 3 on page 13.

Do you need to review the grammar?

Review

- the *present continuous*
- the *present continuous* to talk about the future
- the *past simple* of regular verbs
- comparative adverbs (*better*).

☞ In Exercise 1, choose the correct answer (A or B).

In **recording 🎧 5 🎧** (page 44), you will hear the information.

Remember: listen for the information about the correct time (*present, past, ...*).

☞ In Exercise 2, complete the answers.

In **recording 🎧 6 🎧** (page 44), you will hear the information.

Remember: you will have time to write your answer after each conversation.

☞ In Exercise 3, write the answers.

In **recording 🎧 7 🎧** (page 45), you will hear the information.

Remember: you will have time to write your answer after each conversation.

- Only give short answers.

1. **Listen to** recording 🎧5🎧 **and tick A or B for each question.**

    1. How is Nick doing in French this year?

      A ☐ Well.   **B** ☐ OK.

    2. How were Nick's results last year?

      A ☐ Better.   **B** ☐ Same.

    3. What does Nick need to improve?

      A ☐ His enthusiasm.   **B** ☐ His speaking.

2. **Listen to** recording 🎧6🎧 **and complete each answer.**

    1. What does Nick need to do?

      _____ to French people.

    2. Do any French people live in the same area as the Green family?

      _____ they do.

    3. What does Mr Green want to do?

      _____ a CD.

3. **Listen to** recording 🎧7🎧 **and answer the questions.**

    1. Where is Monsieur Blanc taking a group of students next year?

      _____

    2. Where did the students stay last year?

      _____

    3. Did the students' French improve?

      _____

Activities for *Quickmarch* Task 3

It helps to know lots of words and grammar points to do these *Reading* and *Writing* exercises. Ask your teacher or parent to help you.

Remember:

- Read the instructions carefully.
- Think about the words you need.
- Check your answers.

TOP TIPS

First, read the conversations carefully.

- What is the dialogue about?
- What kinds of questions are they?
  If the answer is *yes* or *no*, the question is a **closed question** (for example, *Was it good?*).
  If the answer gives more information or an opinion, the question is an **open question** (for example, *Who did you go with?*).

In English, questions starting with *Wh-* are always open questions. (*Who, What, Where, ...*).

- Is your question in the right order: QASI (*Question word – Auxiliary – Subject – Infinitive*)?

Do Exercises 1, 2 and 3 on page 15.

Do you need to review the grammar?

Review

- question words
- question tags.

☞ In Exercise 1, complete the sentences.

Remember: check if you need a question word (*Where ..., Who ...*) or an auxiliary verb (*Did ..., Are ..., Can ...*)?

When you need an auxiliary in a question, it is usually in the answer also!

For example: *Can you ...? Yes, I can.*

☞ In Exercise 2, complete the beginning of the questions.

Remember:

- Look at the answers first.
- Use *How* to ask about an action.

☞ In Exercise 3, complete the end of the questions.

Remember: make sure the question makes sense and is complete.

- Look at the answers first.
- Underline the important information in the answer.
- Ask a question about that information.

1. Write one question word from the box below in each space in the questions (1–5).

| Who · Did · Are · Where · Was |

Nick: (1) _____ you go on the school trip to France last year?

Justin: Yes, I did.

Nick: (2) _____ it good?

Justin: No, it was brilliant!

Nick: (3) _____ did you go with?

Justin: With some kids from my class and Years 4 and 5.

Nick: (4) _____ did you stay?

Justin: At this really cool campsite. There was an enormous swimming pool!

Nick: (5) _____ you going again this year?

Justin: Definitely. I can't wait!

Nick asks an older boy from school, Justin, to tell him about the school trip to France.

2. Complete these questions (1–5) with the correct question word or auxiliary verb.

Nick: (1) _____ did you get to France?

Justin: We travelled by coach and ferry.

Nick: (2) _____ it take a long time?

Justin: Yes, it did. Almost twelve hours.

Nick: (3) _____ you bored on the coach for all that time?

Justin: Yes, I was. Bored and hungry!

Nick: (4) _____ did you sleep?

Justin: On the coach. It was really uncomfortable!

Nick: (5) _____ you going by coach again this year?

Justin: Yes, we are. It's too expensive to fly.

3. Complete these questions (1–5) in full.

Nick: So, Justin, did (1) _____ ?

Justin: Yes, I did. I know lots of new French words now. Especially for food.

Nick: Was (2) _____ ?

Justin: No, not really. I prefer English and Mexican food.

Nick: And did (3) _____ ?

Justin: Yes, we visited museums, art galleries, the beach and the local hospital.

Nick: Why (4) _____ ?

Justin: My friend, Jimmy, had a terrible earache.

Nick: Is Jimmy (5) _____ ?

Justin: No, he isn't! He's going to Turkey next year.

Activities for *Quickmarch* Task 4

It helps to know lots of words and grammar points to do these *Reading* and *Matching* exercises. Ask your teacher or parent to help you.

Remember:

- Read the instructions carefully.
- Look for words that describe things or actions you see in the pictures.
- There are two extra sentences.
- Check your answers.

TOP TIPS

First, look at the pictures.

- What do you see in the picture?
- Who do you see?
- What is happening?
- Pay attention to the details.

Do Exercises 1 and 2 on page 17.

Do you need to review the grammar?

Review

- the *present simple*
- the *past simple*
- the *imperative*.

Think about these topics:

- *the time*
- *places*.

☞ In Exercise 1, choose the correct picture (A or B).

Remember: read what people say, and choose the picture that matches it.

- Sentence 1 – Mr Green is asking about the place (*Where*).   ✔

    He isn't asking about the time.   ✘

- Sentence 2 – The man points to the lift.   ✔

- Sentence 3 – The welcome meeting starts at 9.00. It doesn't start at 11.00.   ✘

- Sentence 4 – Mrs Green wants *a cup of tea*. She doesn't want to eat.   ✘

- Sentence 5 – Nick says *o'clock*. We only use *o'clock* to talk about the time.   ✘

☞ In Exercise 2, match each sentence to the correct picture.

Remember: read what people say, and choose the picture that matches it.

- Look at what is happening. Pay attention to the details.
- Where is Monsieur Blanc?
- What is he doing in picture C?

1. Read the sentences (1–5). Tick picture A or B for each sentence.

1. Good afternoon. Where is the Study in France exhibition?

2. It's on the top floor. The lift is over there.

3. The welcome meeting starts at 9 o'clock.

4. It's a quarter to nine now. Let's have a cup of tea first.

5. It's nine o'clock, Dad!

2. Read the sentences (1–7). Match each sentence to the correct picture (A–E). Be careful. There are two extra sentences.

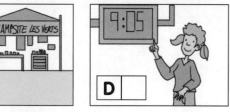

1. Dad, we're late. The presentation started five minutes ago.

2. Let's sit down over there.

3. Look, there's Monsieur Blanc.

4. Hello, Monsieur Blanc. How are you?

5. I'm going to tell everyone about our experience at Les Verts last year!

6. Look, Dad!: Monsieur Blanc is on the stage.

7. Don't forget to look at the campsite stand.

Activities for *Quickmarch* Task 5

It helps to know lots of words and topics to do these *Reading* and *Writing* exercises. Ask your teacher or parent to help you.

Remember:

- Read the instructions carefully.
- Choose the correct form of the verb.
- Check your answers.

TOP TIPS

First, read the text and the verbs in the box.

- What is the text about?
- Which verbs in the box complete the sentences?
- Are these regular or irregular verbs?
- Have you followed the spelling rules?

Do Exercises 1, 2 and 3 on page 19.

Do you need to review the grammar?

Review

- the *past simple*
- regular and irregular verbs.

Think about these topics:

- *spare time*
- *transport.*

☞ In Exercise 1, write each verb in the correct column.

Remember: there are six verbs for each column. If you're not sure, check the list of irregular verbs on pages 6 and 7.

☞ In Exercise 2, underline the correct verbs.

Remember: use the *past simple* because Nick has arrived: the journey is over.

- Only one verb is correct.
- Check the spelling rules on page 7.

☞ In Exercise 3, complete the sentences with the verbs in the box.

Remember: you need to write the verbs in the *past simple*, because both Nick's journey and Olivia's sleepover at Gemma's home were in the past.

- Match each verb to its subject.

Nick goes on the school trip to France. He wants to send an email to Mum, Dad and Olivia to tell them about the journey.

1. **Look at the verbs in the box. Write each verb in the correct column:**

have · play · study · go · talk · sleep
listen · eat · learn · phone · order · make

REGULAR	IRREGULAR

2. **Now help Nick to finish his email to his family. Underline the correct verbs.**

Dear Mum, Dad and Olivia!
How are you all? I'm here in France.
It (1) **is/was/were** a long journey on the coach. I (2) **sleep/sleeped/slept** for a lot of the time and then (3) **play/plays/played** video games with my friends. We (4) **study/studyed/studied** some more French, too, and (5) **order/orders/ordered** our lunch in French on the ferry. I (6) **have/haved/had** chicken and chips – not very French, but delicious!
See you all soon.

Love,

Nick

3. **Olivia wants to reply to Nick. Help her to finish her email. Use the verbs in the box.**

eat · have · go · is
listen · sleep

Hi Nick,
Thanks for your email!
Your journey sounds like it (1) _____ really boring!
I (2) _____ a great weekend. I (3) _____ over at Gemma's house and we (4) _____ to music all evening. We (5) _____ pizza and chips for dinner and we (6) _____ to bed really late!
Write soon with some exciting news!

Lots of love,

Olivia

Activities for *Quickmarch* Task 6

It helps to know lots of words and grammar points to do these *Writing* exercises. Ask your teacher or parent to help you.

Remember:

- Read the instructions carefully.
- Think about the information you need.
- Check your answers.

TOP TIPS

First, read the sentences.

- How do the sentences begin?
- Which words do you know about this topic?

Do Exercises 1, 2 and 3 on page 21.

Do you need to review the grammar?

Review

- the *present simple*
- the *past simple*
- the *future* (*going to* and the *present continuous*)
- *adverbs of frequency*.

Think about this topic:

- *transport*.

☞ In Exercise 1, write six words about travel.

Remember: there are no right or wrong answers. Write words you remember well and can spell correctly.

- Examples for travel and transport: *train, bus, plane, bike, car, ferry, boat, ...*

☞ In Exercise 2, tick the correct answers for you. Then complete the last column.

Remember: there are no right or wrong answers. This exercise prepares you for the *Writing* exercise.

☞ In Exercise 3, complete the sentences.

Remember: you have to write about 50 words in total, but do not take too much time counting them. That's about 10 words for each sentence!

Examples:

1. *I go to school on foot with my friends.*
2. *Travelling by bike is fun, but sometimes the roads are dangerous. I always wear my helmet.*
3. *I think train journeys are exciting and more fun than travelling by car.*
4. *Last year I went to the beach for my holidays. We got the bus from my town.*
5. *Next summer I'm going to Thailand for my holidays. We're going to visit my aunt in Bangkok.*

1. Complete this mind map. Write six words connected to travel.

2. Look at the table. Tick the correct answers for you, then complete the last column with other information.

How do you get to school?	☐ by car	☐ by bus	☐ on foot	other information: _____
Can you ride a bike?	☐ yes	☐ no	☐ not good	other information: _____
Do you like train journeys?	☐ yes	☐ no	☐ I don't know	other information: _____
Did you go anywhere by plane last year?	☐ yes to: _____	☐ no	☐ I don't remember	other information: _____
Are you going on any big trips next summer?	☐ yes to: _____	☐ no	☐ I don't remember	other information: _____

3. Complete the sentences about the journeys you make.

1. I go to school _____ .

2. Travelling by bike is _____ .

3. I think train journeys are _____ .

4. Last year I _____ .

5. Next summer I'm _____ .

Activities for *Quickmarch Speaking* Task 7

The *Speaking* exercises can be difficult. Ask your teacher or parent to help you.

Remember:

- Listen to the examiner's instructions.
- Always ask and answer questions in sentences.
- Show the examiner that you know the grammar and vocabulary.
- Ask the examiner if you do not understand something.

TOP TIPS

First, look at the pictures and read the cards.

- What do you see in the picture?
- Can you pronounce the question on the card?
- Can you answer the question?

Remember: count out loud in English as you move from square to square on the board game!

Do Exercises 1, 2 and 3 on page 23.

Do you need to review the grammar and vocabulary?

See the list on page 8. What topics do you need to study?

☞ In Exercise 1, match the questions to the correct answers.

- Look for auxiliary verbs in the question, such as *Do ... Can ...* in the question: you will also find it in the answer!

☞ In Exercise 3, answer the questions on the cards.

A *Where are you from?*

B *When was the last time you went to the cinema?*

C *What are you going to do this weekend?*

D *Who is the oldest person in your family?*

E *Where did you go on holiday last summer?*

F *Are you meeting your friends later?*

Remember: in English, **open questions** always start with *Wh - [Wh-]* (*Who, What, Where, ...*).

You can reply as you like.

Closed questions start with *Have you ..., Can you ...* or *Are you .....* . The start of the answer has to have *Yes* or *No*.

Then, you can add more information.

1. Nick meets a French girl, Marianne, on the school trip. Match Nick's questions (1–6) to Marianne's answers (A–F).

1.	Do you live here?	**A**	Yes, with my Mum and two sisters.
2.	When did you arrive?	**B**	Nothing. Just hanging out.
3.	Did you come with your family?	**C**	No, I don't. I'm on holiday.
4.	Can you sail?	**D**	OK. See you about 11.00?
5.	What are you doing tomorrow?	**E**	Last Saturday.
6.	Do you want to meet at the beach?	**F**	Yes, I can. We've got a small boat.

2. Work with a partner. Imagine you are on holiday. Ask and answer the questions in Exercise 1. Make sure you change the answers!

3. Look at these squares from a board game. Work with a partner. Ask and answer the questions.

Where are you from?

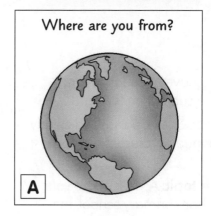

A

When was the last time you went to the cinema?

B

What are you going to do this weekend?

C

Who is the oldest person in your family?

D

Where did you go on holiday last summer?

E

Are you meeting your friends later?

F

Activities for *Quickmarch Speaking* Task 8

The *Speaking* exercises can be difficult. Ask your teacher or parent to help you.

Remember:

- Listen carefully to the examiner's instructions.
- Show the examiner that you know the grammar and vocabulary.
- Ask the examiner if you do not understand something.

TOP TIPS

First, look at the picture on the topic card and read the topic carefully.

- What do you see in the picture?
- What do you need to talk about?
- What grammar and vocabulary do you need to talk about it?

Remember: you have to pay attention to the pronunciation!

Do Exercises 1, 2, 3 and 4 on page 25.

Do you need to review the grammar and vocabulary?

Review

- see the list on page 8 – which topics do you need to study more?

☞ In Exercise 1, **match the two parts of the sentences.**

Remember: look for information that completes the sentence.

☞ In Exercise 3, **write two sentences.**

Here are some suggestions:

A   *My grandma was a teacher in London.*
B   *I love sushi, but my mum doesn't like it.*
C   *I always ride my bike to school.*
D   *I can sing really well, but I can't dance or play a musical instrument.*
E   *I want to study history at university when I'm older.*
F   *I'm going to the seaside with my family in July.*

☞ In Exercise 4, **you will talk about these topics:**

A   My school friends
B   My next holiday
C   My special talents
D   My last meal
E   The last film I saw
F   My plans for the weekend

Remember: you have to speak for one minute about the subject on the card.

Do not go too fast. Speak slowly and clearly. Use different language (*present simple, past simple, future*).

- Example for **topic A**: Talk about your best friend from primary school, the friends you have now, ...
- Example for **topic B**: Talk about where you want to go / where you are going, the type of holiday you like, who you go with, what you do, ...
- Example for **topic C**: Talk about what you are very good at, what you want to do well, your interests and achievements.
- Example for **topic D**: Talk about what you ate for your last meal. Was it nice or disgusting? Who made the meal? Who did you eat it with?
- Example for **topic E**: Talk about the last film that you watched. Was it on TV? Did you go to the cinema? Who did you watch the film with?
- Example for **topic F**: Talk about your weekend. Are you going to stay at home and study? Are you going to go out with your family or friends?

1. Nick has to give a presentation to his class about his trip to France. Match the sentence halves (1–6) and (A–F) from Nick's presentation. Draw lines.

1. I went on the trip	**A** better French now.
2. We travelled	**B** to the South of France.
3. I ate a lot of	**C** new friends.
4. I made some	**D** by coach and ferry.
5. I can speak	**E** chips and ice-cream.
6. I'm going to go	**F** back there again next year.

2. Write each phrase from Exercise 1 in the correct topic box.

A PEOPLE
_____
_____
_____

B FOOD
_____
_____
_____

C TRANSPORT
_____
_____
_____

D ABILITY
_____
_____
_____

E FUTURE
_____
_____
_____

F HOLIDAYS
_____
_____
_____

3. Add two more sentences to each box.

4. Look at these topic cards. Work with a partner. Talk for one minute about each topic.

A

My school friends

B

My next holiday

C

My special talents

D

My last meal

E

The last film I saw

F

My plans for the weekend

Can you do all of these things in English?

	Yes	No
• Talk and ask about sports and hobbies.	☐	☐
• Talk and ask about everyday activities.	☐	☐
• Talk and ask about countries, cities, towns, shops and buildings.	☐	☐
• Talk and ask about modes of transport and journeys.	☐	☐
• Order food in a restaurant.	☐	☐
• Talk about past events.	☐	☐
• Understand, ask and answer questions about a story.	☐	☐
• Understand a simple story.	☐	☐
• Talk about future plans.	☐	☐
• Tell the time (hours and minutes).	☐	☐
• Can you use all the language on page 8?	☐	☐
• Do you know all the vocabulary on page 8?	☐	☐

Mostly "YES":

Hurray! You're ready to take the *Quickmarch* test. Do the past papers on page 48.

Mostly "NO":

Keep trying! Study some more. Complete the study plan on page 27.

My study plan

GRAMMAR

I need to practise this grammar:

_____

_____

_____

_____

VOCABULARY

I need to learn some more words about these topics:

_____

_____

_____

_____

LISTENING - READING - WRITING - SPEAKING

I need to learn how to do these things in English:

_____

_____

_____

_____

Now, do the checklist on page 26 again.

Activities for *Breakthrough* Task 1

The *Listening* exercises can be difficult. Ask your teacher or parent to help you.

Remember:

- Read the instructions carefully.
- Listen to the audio twice.
- Listen for information you need to complete the exercise.
- Only one picture is correct.
- Check your answers.

TOP TIPS

First, look at the pictures.

- Who or what do you see in the picture?
- Where are the people or objects in the picture?
- How do they look?
- What are they doing?
- What other information does the picture show (time, date, ...)?

Do Exercises 1, 2 and 3 on page 29.

Do you need to review the grammar?

Review

- *going to*
- *will*
- the *present perfect*
- *would rather*.

Think about these topics:

- *geography*
- *wild animals*.

☞ In Exercise 1, choose the correct picture (A or B).

In **recording** 8 (page 45), you will hear the mother say how she will book the flight.

Remember: you have to listen for specific details.

- Circle the positive information you hear in the audio (for example: *I'll go to the travel agent's ...*).
- Cross out the negative information in the audio (for example: *No, I've never done it before.*).

☞ In Exercise 2, choose the correct picture (A or B).

In **recording** 9 (page 45), you will hear the information you need.

Remember: only one picture is correct.

☞ In Exercise 3, choose the correct picture (A, B or C).

In **recording** 10 (page 45), you will hear the information you need.

Remember: listen for the keywords (see the highlighted words on page 45).

1. Listen to recording 🎧8🎧 and look at the pictures. Tick picture A or B.

A ☐

B ☐

2. Listen to recording 🎧9🎧 and look at the pictures. Read the questions (1–3) and tick picture A or B.

1. Where does Olivia want to go?

 A ☐

 B ☐

2. Has Olivia ever been to the West coast?

A ☐   B ☐

3. Why does Olivia want to go to Monkey Mia?

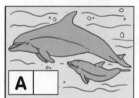 A ☐

 B ☐

3. Listen to recording 🎧10🎧 and look at the pictures. Read the questions (1–3) and tick picture A, B or C.

1. What animals does Nick want to see?

 A ☐

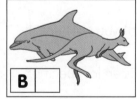 B ☐

 C ☐

2. What would Mum rather do?

 A ☐

 B ☐

 C ☐

3. What will Nick do if he sees a kangaroo?

 A ☐

 B ☐

 C ☐

Activities for *Breakthrough* Task 2

The *Listening* exercises can be difficult. Ask your teacher or parent to help you.

Remember:

- Read the instructions carefully.
- Listen to the audio twice.
- Listen for information you need to complete the exercise.
- The conversation is in parts.
- Only write short answers.
- Check your answers.

TOP TIPS

First, read the questions.

- Is the question about *who* or *what*?
- What information should you listen for (a time, a place, a name)?
- Do you need information about the past, the present or the future?

Do Exercises 1, 2 and 3 on page 31.

Do you need to review the grammar?

Review

- the *present continuous*
- the *present continuous* to talk about the future
- *will.*

Think about this topic:

- *the time.*

☞ In Exercise 1, choose the correct answer (A or B).

In **recording** 🎧11 (page 45), you will hear the details.

Remember: you have to listen for specific information.

- Make sure you listen to the information about the correct time (*present, past* or *future*).

☞ In Exercise 2, complete the answers.

In **recording** 🎧12 (page 46), you will hear the information.

Remember: you will have time to write your answer after each conversation.

☞ In Exercise 3, write the answers.

In **recording** 🎧13 (page 46), you will hear the information.

Remember: you will have time to write your answer after each conversation.

- Only write short answers.

1. Listen to recording 🎧11 and tick A or B for each question (1–3).

    1. When will they get to Singapore?

        A ☐ In 13 hours.   **B** ☐ Don't know.

    2. What time is it?

        A ☐ 10 o'clock.   **B** ☐ 1 o'clock.

    3. Why has Olivia got the headphones?

        A ☐ To watch a film.   **B** ☐ To listen to music.

2. Listen to recording 🎧12 and complete the answers (1–3).

    1. Can Olivia fly the plane?

        _____ she can't but she can sit in the co-pilot's chair.

    2. If the pilot presses the red button, will the plane go faster?

        _____ , it won't.

    3. What will happen if the pilot presses the red button?

        _____ will bring him a cup of tea.

3. Listen to recording 🎧13 and answer the questions (1–3).

    1. What is Nick doing?

        _____

    2. What does Olivia decide to do?

        _____

    3. Why does Nick decide to play another game?

        _____

Activities for *Breakthrough* Task 3

It helps to know lots of words and grammar points to do these *Reading* and *Writing* exercises. Ask your teacher or parent to help you.

Remember:

- Read the instructions carefully.
- Think about the words you need.
- Check your answers.

TOP TIPS

First, read the conversation.

- What is the dialogue about?
- What kinds of questions are they?

If the answer is *Yes* or *No*, the question is a **closed question** (for example, *Have you ever been surfing?*).

If the answer gives more information or an opinion, the question is an **open question** (for example, *How was the first flight to Singapore?*).

In English, questions starting with *Wh-* are always open questions. The answer to a *Wh-*question is never *Yes* or *No*.

- Is your question in the right order: QASI (*Question word – Auxilary – Subject – Infinitive*)?

Do Exercises 1, 2 and 3 on page 33.

Do you need to review the grammar?

Review

- question words
- question tags.

Think about this topic:

- *spare time.*

☞ In Exercise 1, complete the questions with words from the box.

Remember: check if you need one question word (*What ...*, *How ...*) or an auxiliary verb (*It's ...*, *Would ...*)?

When you need an auxiliary verb in a question it is usually in the answer as well! For example, **Can** you ...? Yes, I **can**.

- Question tags confirm something that we already know. Do you remember how to use them?

☞ In Exercise 2, complete the beginning of the questions.

Remember: look at the answers first.

☞ In Exercise 3, write the questions.

Remember: the question must make sense and be complete.

- Look at the answers first.
- Underline the key information in the answer.
- Ask a question about that information.

1. Write one word from the box below in each space in questions (1–5).

What · How · Would · What · It's

Tom: (1) _____ was the first flight to Singapore?

Nick: It was OK, but really long.

Tom: (2) _____ time is your next flight?

Nick: In about two hours, at four o'clock.

Tom: (3) _____ are you going to do for the next two hours?

Nick: I've got my PlayStation, so I'll play on that.

Tom: (4) _____ lucky you brought it, isn't it?

Nick: Yeah! I love my PlayStation!

Tom: (5) _____ you rather go to sleep when you get here or go out?

Nick: Let's go out, to the beach!

Tom texts Nick to find out how the journey is going.

2. Tom asks Nick if he wants to try surfing. Complete these questions (1–5) with the correct question word or auxiliary verb.

Tom: (1) _____ you ever been surfing?

Nick: No, but I want to try it.

Tom: (2) _____ you like me to ask my friend Jack to lend you his surfboard?

Nick: Yes, please. That would be great!

Tom: (3) _____ you think you'll be good at surfing?

Nick: I hope so!

Tom: (4) _____ you scared of sharks?

Nick: Sharks?! Yes, I'm scared of them! If I see a shark, I'll scream!

Tom: (5) _____ really scream, will you? That would be so embarrassing!

Nick: Yes, I will, I've never seen a real shark!

3. Tom asks Nick what he wants to do on his first day in Sydney. Write the questions (1–5) in full.

Tom: (1) _____ ?

Nick: I really want to go to the beach.

Tom: (2) _____ ?

Nick: Yes, I'd love to visit the stadium. Let's go to the beach in the morning and then the stadium after lunch.

Tom: (3) _____ ?

Nick: Yes! We can have a sandwich on the beach for lunch and then the barbecue in the evening.

Tom: (4) _____ ?

Nick: Kangaroo meat?! No, I haven't!

Tom: (5) _____ ?

Nick: No, I won't! I refuse to eat kangaroo!

Activities for *Breakthrough* Task 4

It helps to know lots of words and grammar points to do these *Reading* and *Matching* exercises. Ask your teacher or parent to help you.

Remember:

- Read the instructions carefully.
- Look for words about the objects or actions you see in the pictures.
- There are two extra sentences.
- Check your answers.

TOP TIPS

First, look at the pictures.

- What do you see in the picture?
- Who do you see?
- What is happening?
- Pay attention to the details.

Do Exercises 1, 2 and 3 on page 35.

Do you need to review the grammar?

Review

- the *present perfect*
- the *first conditional*.

Think about these topics:

- *holidays*
- *airports*.

☞ In Exercise 1, choose the correct picture (A or B) for each sentence.

Remember: read what people say, and choose the picture that matches it.

Pay attention to the keywords!

- Sentence 1 – *passport*
- Sentence 2 – *I've messaged*
- Sentence 3 – *Can we get ...?*
- Sentence 4 – *get our suitcases*

☞ In Exercise 2, match the sentence to the correct picture.

Remember: read what people say, and choose the picture that matches it.

- Look at what is happening. Pay attention to the details.
- Read sentence 4: can you see the airport employee with the phone in his hand in one of the pictures?

1. Read the sentences (1–4). Tick picture A or B for each sentence.

1. Good afternoon. Where is Passport Control, please?

 A  B

2. I've messaged Tom to tell him we're here.

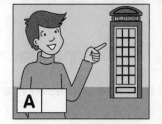 A  B

3. Mum, I'm really thirsty. Can we get some water?

 A  B

4. Would you rather get our suitcases first or go to the bathroom first?

 A  B

2. Read the sentences (1–6). Match each sentence (1–6) to the correct picture (A–D). Be careful. There are two extra sentences.

 A  B

 C D

1. Excuse me, but our suitcases haven't arrived.

2. Have you checked the right carousel?

3. That black case over there isn't yours, is it?

4. If your suitcases arrive later, we'll call you immediately.

5. Go through the door to the Arrivals gate.

6. If they don't arrive, we'll find them. Don't worry!

Activities for *Breakthrough* Task 5

It helps to know lots of words and grammar points to do these *Reading* and *Writing* exercises. Ask your teacher or parent to help you.
Remember:
- Read the instructions carefully.
- Think about what kind of word you need for each space. (verb, noun, ...)
- Write **only one word** in each space.
- Check your answers.

TOP TIPS

First, read the text and the words in the box.
- What is the text about?
- Which words can you use to complete the sentences?
- Pay attention to spelling.

Do Exercises 1, 2 and 3 on page 37.
Do you need to review the grammar?
See the list of topics on page 9. Which topics do you need to think about?

☞ In Exercise 1, write each word in the correct column.

Remember: there are two words for each column. If you're not sure, check your dictionary.

☞ In Exercise 2, correct the words.
Remember: only one of the words is correct.

☞ In Exercise 3, complete the sentences with one word in each space.

1. **Olivia writes an email to her best friend Francesca about her first day in Sydney.**

   Look at the words in the box. Write each word in the correct column.

   > surfboard · always · sunny · quickly · exciting
   > we · ran · beach · his · went

VERBS	NOUNS	ADJECTIVES	PRONOUNS	ADVERBS

2. **Now help Olivia to start her email to Francesca. Underline the correct words.**

   Hi Francesca!

   I can't believe it! We're actually here in Sydney. Yesterday we (1) **go/went** to the beach. Tom (2) **always/never** goes there with his friends and they go surfing. The weather was beautiful – it was really (3) **rainy/sunny**. Tom's friend let me use his (4) **surfboard/skateboard** so that I could try surfing too. Then (5) **I/we** practised on the sand first before I went into the ocean. It was so (6) **excited/exciting**.

3. **Olivia wants to finish her email. Fill in the gaps.**

   I quickly learned what to do but it (1) _____ really difficult.
   When the waves (2) _____ , I tried to surf them, but usually fell off my board. I need (3) _____ practise then I'll get better but I'll never be as (4) _____ as Tom and (5) _____ friends.
   I'll (6) _____ you some photos soon!

   Lots of love.

   Olivia xxx

Activities for *Breakthrough* Task 6

It helps to know lots of words and grammar points to do these *Reading* and *Writing* exercises. Ask your teacher or parent to help you.

Remember:

- Read the instructions carefully.
- Look at what happens in each picture.
- Imagine the story.
- Write the story in no more than 75 words.
- You have to use all of the pictures.
- Check the grammar, spelling and punctuation in your story.

TOP TIPS

First, look at the pictures.

- Who are the characters?
- What are the most important events?
- What else happens?

Do Exercises 1, 2 and 3 on page 39.

Do you need to review the grammar?

Review

- the *past simple*
- the *past continuous.*

Think about this topic:

- *seaside.*

☞ In Exercise 1, circle the main event in red and the other event in blue.

Remember: the main events of a story are in the *past simple*. Other events that happen at the same time are in the *past continuous.*

☞ In Exercise 2, match the pictures to the correct sentences in Exercise 1.

Remember: you have to use all of the sentences.

☞ In Exercise 3, write Olivia's story.

Remember: you need to use all of the sentences.

- Write what Olivia was doing and what also happened at the same time.

1. **Look at the sentences in the box. Circle each underlined part of the sentence: the MAIN EVENT in red, the simple HAPPENING in blue.**

    1. I was walking along the beach when I saw a lot of people near the water.

    2. I was asking Olivia about the group of people when I heard Nick screaming.

    3. I phoned for help while I ran down to the sea.

    4. I swam into the water while I shouted to the lifeguard.

2. **Match the pictures (A–D) to the sentences (1–4) in Exercise 1.**

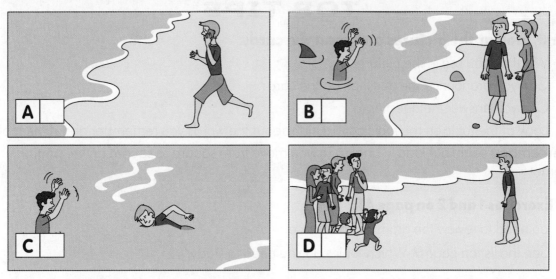

3. **Look at the pictures (A–D). Write Olivia's story about what happened at the beach.**

_____

_____

_____

_____

_____

Activities for *Breakthrough Speaking* Tasks 7 and 8

The *Speaking* exercises can be difficult. Ask your teacher or parent to help you.

Remember:

- Listen carefully to the examiner's instructions.
- Always ask and answer questions in sentences.
- Show the examiner that you know the grammar and vocabulary.
- Ask the examiner if you do not understand something.

TOP TIPS

First, look at the pictures and read the cards.

- What do you see in the picture?
- Can you pronounce the question on the card?
- Can you answer the question?
- Look at the topic on the topic card. Think about the words you remember about the topic.

Remember: count out loud in English as you move from square to square on the board game!

Do Exercises 1 and 2 on page 41.

Do you need to review the grammar and vocabulary?

- See the list on page 9. Which topics do you need to study?

☞ In Exercise 1, ask and answer the questions.

A *Have you ever been to Australia?*

B *Would you rather spend your summer holidays by the sea or in the mountains?*

C *When was the last time you cried?*

D *What will you do if it rains this weekend?*

Remember: try to pronounce the words correctly. For example, if you say something in the plural, make the s sound clearly at the end of the word.

☞ In Exercise 2, talk about these topics:

A *The last time I was sick.*

B *All about space travel.*

C *The most beautiful place in the world.*

D *How to protect endangered species.*

Remember: you have to speak for one minute. Do not go too fast. Speak slowly and clearly.

- Example for **topic A:** *Talk about something you know (I had a fever last month ...).*
- Example for **topic B:** *Talk about living on another planet in the future (I would rather live on Mars with my family ...).*
- Example for **topic C:** *Talk about a wonderful view you remember (My favourite place in the world is the view of the mountains from my house ...).*
- Example for **topic D:** *Talk about habitats (Forests are very important for wild animals ...).*

1. Look at these squares from a board game. Work with a partner. Ask and answer the questions.

Have you ever been to Australia?

A

Would you rather spend your summer holidays by the sea or in the mountains?

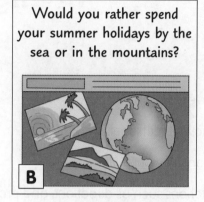

B

When was the last time you cried?

C

What will you do if it rains this weekend?

D

2. Look at these topic cards. Work with a partner. Talk for one minute about each topic.

A

The last time I was sick

B

All about space travel

C

The most beautiful place in the world

D

How to protect endangered species

Can you do all of these things in English?

	Yes	No
• Describe everyday objects.	☐	☐
• Describe how objects feel.	☐	☐
• Describe sensations.	☐	☐
• Give instructions such as directions and procedures.	☐	☐
• Write a story/narrative about a special event.	☐	☐
• Talk about past experiences.	☐	☐
• Ask for/give explanations and express purpose.	☐	☐
• Ask for/give opinions.	☐	☐
• Ask about/state preferences.	☐	☐
• Predict and discuss future possibility.	☐	☐
• Can you use all the language on page 9?	☐	☐
• Do you know all the vocabulary on page 9?	☐	☐

Mostly "YES":

Hurray! You're ready to take the *Breakthrough* test. Do the past papers on page 64.

Mostly "NO":

Keep trying! Study some more. Complete the study plan on page 43.

My study plan

GRAMMAR

I need to practise this grammar:

_____

_____

_____

_____

VOCABULARY

I need to learn some more words about these topics:

_____

_____

_____

_____

LISTENING – READING – WRITING – SPEAKING

I need to learn how to do these things in English:

_____

_____

_____

_____

Now, do the checklist on page 42 again.

Audio scripts

Recording 🎧2🎧 (pages 10–11)

Olivia: I really want to go to Florida next summer.

Nick: America? No way! I want to go and see Tom in Australia.

Olivia: I want to see Tom too. He can come to America.

Nick: No, he can't. It's too expensive. And, I want to go and see the kangaroos.

Olivia: Yeah, and don't forget the crocodiles. Urgh! I'm scared of crocodiles!

Nick: I don't like the crocodiles, but there are crocodiles in Florida too, Olivia.

Olivia: OK, let's go to Sydney! There are no crocodiles in Sydney!

Recording 🎧3🎧 (pages 10–11)

Olivia: Let's go and see Tom in August. We can stay for four weeks.

Nick: It's winter in Australia in August and I want to go surfing. It's hot in January.

Olivia: But Tom visited us in August.

Nick: Yes, but just for two weeks. His big school holidays are in December.

Olivia: OK, let's tell Mum we want to go for our winter holidays.

Nick: Fantastic.

Olivia: Hmm… so what are we going to do this summer?

Recording 🎧4🎧 (pages 10–11)

Nick: Mum, can we go to Australia for our winter holidays?

Mum: Are you crazy? They are in three weeks. We haven't got plane tickets.

Olivia: Please, Mum. It's hot and sunny in Sydney now.

Mum: We're going to Scotland for our winter holidays with Auntie Jill and Uncle Pete.

Nick: But Mum, we went to Scotland last year for our winter holidays!

Mum: Scotland is beautiful. Maybe we can go to Australia next year.

Olivia: OK!

Recording 🎧5🎧 (pages 12–13)

M. Blanc: Good evening, Mr Green. Please, sit down.

Mr Green: Thank you, Monsieur Blanc.

M. Blanc: So, let's talk about Nick's progress this year.

Mr Green: Is he doing well?

M. Blanc: He's doing OK.

_____

Mr Green: Only OK?

M. Blanc: Yes, his results were better last year.

_____

Mr Green: Really? Nick always says that he loves French.

M. Blanc: Yes, he's very enthusiastic, but he needs to practise his speaking more.

Recording 🎧6🎧 (pages 12–13)

Mr Green: So, what can we do to help Nick?

M. Blanc: He needs to speak to French people outside class. Do you have any French friends?

Mr Green: No. We've got some Spanish friends.

_____

M. Blanc: Are there any French people who live in your area?

Mr Green: Hmmm, yes … Olivia was friends with a French girl called Marianne at her dance class.

M. Blanc: Wonderful! You must telephone this family. Invite them for dinner!

Mr Green: Dinner? Maybe we can just buy a French conversation CD.

Recording 🎧7 (pages 12–13)

M. Blanc: There is something that might help Nick.

Mr Green: What?

M. Blanc: We are taking a group of students to the South of France in July.

_____

Mr Green: Excellent idea!

M. Blanc: Yes, we stayed at the same place last year and the kids loved it.

_____

Mr Green: And did their French improve?

M. Blanc: Yes, it did. They ordered all their snacks at the bar in French.

Mr Green: Brilliant! So could you give me some more information, please?

Recording 🎧8 (pages 28–29)

Olivia: Are you going to book our flights tomorrow, Mum?

Mum: Yes, I'll do it when I finish work.

Nick: Are you going to do it on the Internet?

Mum: No, I've never done it before. I'll go to the travel agent's in town.

Recording 🎧9 (pages 28–29)

Olivia: Mum, can we go to Monkey Mia this time?

Mum: But that's over on the west coast, Olivia. We're going to Sydney, on the east coast.

Olivia: I know, Mum, and I really love Sydney, but I've never been to the other side of Australia and I really want to get in the water with the dolphins.

Mum: Olivia, would you rather spend time with your cousin or with the dolphins?

Olivia: Well...

Mum: OK, don't answer that!

Recording 🎧10 (pages 28–29)

Nick: Mum, I don't want to go all the way to Australia to see dolphins! I want to see kangaroos and crocodiles.

Mum: Those are dangerous animals.

Nick. I'd rather hug a koala!

Nick: Have you ever held a koala, Mum?

Mum: No, I haven't, but if I see one this time, I'll ask for a hug and a photo.

Nick: And if I see a kangaroo, I'll ask for a boxing match!

Recording 🎧11 (pages 30–31)

Nick: Excuse me! What time will we get to Sydney?

F/A*: We've only just taken off.

Nick: I know, but how long does the flight take?

F/A: It's 13 hours to Singapore and then you have to change plane.

_____

Olivia: Are you going to bring lunch soon?

F/A: Erm... lunch is at one o'clock. It's only ten o'clock.

Olivia: I'm starving. Maybe it's lunch time in Australia!

Nick: Have some crisps, Olivia!

_____

Nick: Have you got any headphones, please? I'd like to watch a film.

F/A: Yes, they're in that front compartment.

Nick: I can't find them.

F/A: I think your sister's got them.

Olivia: I want to listen to some reggae music.

Nick: Use your own, Olivia!

* Flight attendant

Recording 12 (pages 30–31)

Pilot: G'day kids, come in, have a look round!

Olivia: This is so cool! Can I try and fly for a minute?

Pilot: Sorry, but that's against the rules. You can sit in the co-pilot's chair though.

_____

Nick: Wow! There are so many buttons and switches.

Pilot: I know, and I have to remember which ones to press at the right time.

Nick: If you press that red one, will we go faster?

Pilot: No!

_____

Nick: What is that button for then?

Pilot: If I press that red button, my colleague will bring me a cup of tea.

Recording 13 (pages 30–31)

Olivia: Nick, what are you going to do on our first day?

Nick: What? I don't know.

Olivia: Come on, Nick! Why don't we go to the beach?

Nick: Olivia, sssh! I'm playing my game.

_____

Olivia: Boring! Why don't we plan our itinerary for the first week?

Nick: Be quiet, Olivia. I can't hear my game.

Olivia: Fine, I'll do my own special events programme.

_____

Nick: OK, I've finished my game now. What do you want to plan?

Olivia: Zzzzzz...

Nick: Oh great! Now Olivia's sleeping! Ah well, time for another game!

Past Papers

Quickmarch Written test

Hello kids, hello boys and girls. Today's test is Quickmarch. Tasks One and Two are listening. Good luck and have fun!!

1. **Task One: Ben's School Trip (14 marks)**

   Ben and his mum, Mrs Brown, are talking about a school trip. Listen to their conversation. After each part of the conversation, answer the question. Put a cross (☒) in the box under the correct picture.

   You will hear the conversation twice. First, listen to the example.

   Example: What time does Ben get home?

A ☐   B ☐   C ☒

1. Which teacher is Mrs King?

A ☐   B ☐   C ☐

2. Where did Ben's class go on their last school trip?

A ☐   B ☐   C ☐

Leave blank

3. Which castle is the class going to visit?

A ☒   B ☒   C ☒

4. When is the trip to the castle?

July 13th   July 14th   July 15th

A ☒   B ☒   C ☒

5. How is Ben going to school on the day of the visit?

A ☒   B ☒   C ☒

6. What do the students need on the trip?

A ☒   B ☒   C ☒

7. What does the trip cost?

£5	£10	£12
A ☒	B ☒	C ☒

Task 1

(Total 14 marks)

Leave blank

2. **Task Two: Leaving for the Castle (16 marks)**

At school, just before the trip, Ben is talking to his teacher, Mrs King. Listen to their conversation.   After each part of the conversation, write a short answer to the question.

You will hear the conversation twice. First, listen to the example.

Example: When is the bus arriving?

in ten minutes
....

1.   How many children are already at the school?

....

2.   Why can't Mary go on the trip?

....

3.   How is Tom coming to school?

....

4.   How long is it going to take to get to the castle?

....

5.   What time does the castle open?

....

6.   How long are the children staying at the castle?

....

7.   Where are the children going to have lunch?

....

8.   Where do the parents need to meet the children?

....

Task 2

(Total 16 marks)

THAT IS THE END OF THE LISTENING TASKS. NOW GO ON TO TASK THREE.

3. **Task Three: Ben Talks to the Guide (15 marks)**

At the castle, Ben asks Mike, the guide, some questions. Write the questions in the spaces.
The first one is an example.

Ben: (example) *Can I ask you some questions?*

Mike: Of course. It's my job to answer questions.

Ben: How old .... ?

Mike: Lodden Castle is 400 years old.

Ben: Does .... ?

Mike: No. Nobody lives here now. It's only for visitors.

Ben: How many .... ?

Mike: Last year? I don't know, but usually there are 200 visitors a day.

Ben: When.. ?

Mike: I started working here years ago – in 1990.

Ben: Are .... ?

Mike: No. Tomorrow is my free day. I don't work on Fridays.

Task 3

(Total 15 marks)

Leave blank

4. **Task Four: On the School Trip (10 marks)**

Look at these situations on the school trip. Draw a line from the pictures to the correct sentences. The first one is an example.

Be careful. There are two extra sentences.

How much did you pay for that?

We had a great time. It was fantastic.

~~Look. Here comes Nick.~~

I'm going to sit at the back of the bus.

Can you take a picture of me in front of this?

Is anybody sitting here?

That's a nice camera.

Don't touch that please. It's very old.

Task 4

(Total 10 marks)

5. Task Five: Ben Writes in his Diary (15 marks)

In the evening Ben writes about the school trip in his diary. Fill in the missing words. Use the verbs in the box below but don't forget to change them to the PAST TENSE because the trip is finished. The first one is an example.

Today my class **(example)** ....visited......... Lodden Castle.

I **(1)**................................... up at eight o'clock and after breakfast Mum

(2)................................... me to school. Tom **(3)**................................... late to school

again (he got up late) and the bus **(4)**................................... after nine o'clock. At the

castle I **(5)**................................... Mike, the guide. I **(6)**................................... to him

a lot and he **(7)**................................... me all about the castle. After that,

I **(8)**................................... a fantastic book in the castle shop.

It **(9)**................................... me five pounds but it is really interesting. On the way home

I **(10)**................................... at my new book.

I am tired now and I am going to sleep well tonight.

buy	leave	~~visit~~	look
	be	wake	cost
tell	meet	speak	take

Task 5

(Total 15 marks)

6. **Task Six: Our School Trips (10 marks)**

Now write about your school trips.

1. Sometimes...
....
....

2. On our last school trip ....
....
....

3. On our next school trip...
....
....

4. Our most exciting school trip ....
....
....

5. It was exciting because...
....
....

Task 6

(Total 10 marks)

TOTAL FOR PAPER: 80 MARKS

THAT IS THE END OF THE TEST

Quickmarch Spoken test

Instructions for the Oral Examiner

Before conducting the oral test the oral examiner must read the guidance notes inside the current version of the booklet "PTE Young Learners Oral Examination Guide". This booklet will be sent to the test centre by email, three weeks before the date of the written examination. If you have any queries, please contact Language Testing Division of Pearson by emailing pltsupport@pearson.com.

Oral Test

The oral test is a compulsory part of the Pearson Test of English Young Learners. Candidates are examined in groups of five by a trained oral examiner who acts as both interviewer and assessor. At each level the oral test lasts 20 minutes and consists of two 10-minute tasks which focus on the language of the level being tested. The oral accounts for 20 marks.

Stages of the Exam

- The candidates do the board game.
- The candidates take turns picking a card from the pack of topic cards and talking about the topic written on it. After each mini-presentation the other candidates and, if needed, the examiner asks the speaker some questions about the topic.

Task 1: The Board Game

- Required: the board game itself (please cut out the squares from the card provided), dice, five coloured counters.

- Lay out the cards in a circle, a line or S-shape.

- Establish the order of turn taking. (E.g. each candidate rolls the dice and the highest scorer goes first).

- The first candidate rolls the dice and moves the appropriate number of squares. The examiner directs the candidate to address the question to another candidate, referred to by name (e.g. "Ask Fatima"). The candidate then reads out the question and the designated candidate answers it. The square is then turned face down to remove it from the game. The turn passes to the next candidate.

- When moving their counters, candidates should count the squares **in English**.

- Each candidate should respond to at least two questions.

The test is over when each candidate has responded to at least two questions. The game should last no longer than 10 minutes for a group of five candidates.

Task 2: Short Talks

The pack of topic cards is placed face down in the middle of the playing area. The first candidate turns over a card and reads the topic written on it. He or she then speaks about that topic for one minute. At the end of one minute the examiner asks the candidate to stop and invites the other candidates to ask follow-up questions, which the first candidate answers. This continues for one minute (giving the candidate a total turn of two minutes' duration). If the other candidates cannot think of any questions, or if they dry up before the minute is up, the examiner should ask questions. The turn then passes to the next candidate.

Quickmarch cards for board game

What did you do on your last birthday?

How did you come to school today?

What subjects did you have yesterday?

What is the biggest shop near your house?

What do you think is the best sport in the world?

What kind of weather do you like?

What sports are your mum and dad good at?

What time did school start today?

What are you going to do tonight?

Where is your family going to on holiday this year?

What did you watch on TV yesterday?

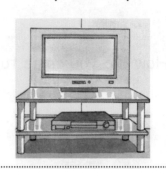

How much homework did you do yesterday?

Which are better – winter holidays or summer holidays?

What are you going to do this weekend?

How many cinemas are there near your house?

How many times a day do you clean your teeth?

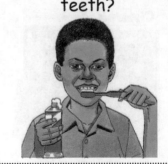

What time do you go to bed in the school holidays?

Where did you go for your last holiday?

Who is the best teacher in your school?

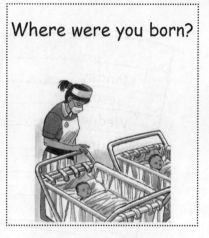

Where were you born?

Quickmarch topic cards

My last school trip

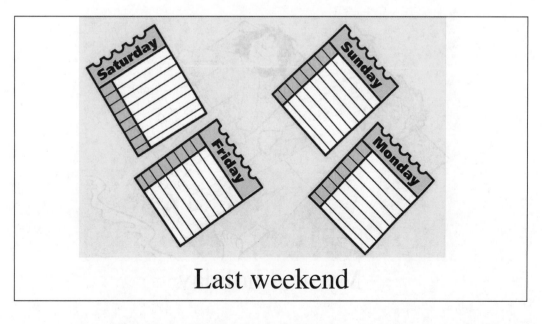

Last weekend

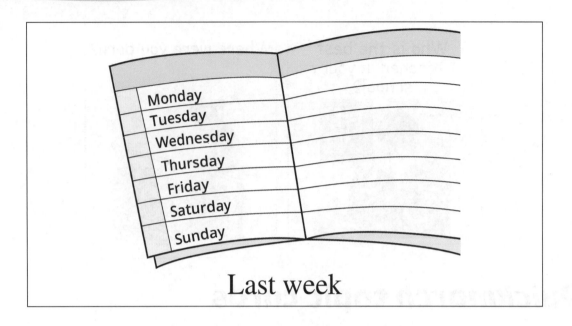

Monday
Tuesday
Wednesday
Thursday
Friday
Saturday
Sunday

Last week

My last birthday

My next holiday

After the test

My most expensive clothes

Tomorrow

My next birthday

Some of my friends

My last time at a restaurant

My last time at a party

MORNING?
AFTERNOON?
EVENING?

My favourite time of day

The best places in my town (city)

Breakthrough Written test

Leave blank

Hello kids, hello boys and girls. Today's test is Breakthrough. Tasks One and Two are listening. Good luck and have fun!!

1. **Task One: A Picnic with Friends (16 marks)**

    Mrs Brown talks about a picnic with her children. Listen to their conversation. After each part of the conversation, answer the question. Put a cross ($\boxtimes$) in the box under the correct picture.

    You will hear the conversation twice. First, listen to the example.

    Example: Where is Mrs Brown?

    A $\boxtimes$ B $\boxtimes$ C $\boxtimes$

1. When was the Browns' last picnic?

    A $\boxtimes$ B $\boxtimes$ C $\boxtimes$

2. Which boy is Mark?

    A $\boxtimes$ B $\boxtimes$ C $\boxtimes$

3. What sport is Mark best at?

A ☒   B ☒   C ☒

4. Which job does Donna's Dad have now?

$x + 2y = 3z$

A ☒   B ☒   C ☒

5. How many friends will the Brown children invite to the picnic?

1   **2**   **3**

A ☒   B ☒   C ☒

6. If it rains, where will the Browns eat?

PARK CAFÉ

A ☒   B ☒   C ☒

7. What food does Ben like best?

A ☒   B ☒   C ☒

8. What has Mrs Brown already bought to drink?

A ☒   B ☒   C ☒

Task 1

(Total 16 marks)

2. **Task Two: Liz Brown Phones a Friend (14 marks)**

The next day Liz Brown phones her friend, Mary, about the picnic. Listen to their conversation. After each part of the conversation, write a short answer to the question.

You will hear the conversation twice. First, listen to the example.

Example: Who answers the phone?

Claire

....

1. Where was Mary when Liz Brown phoned?

....

2. What was Mary doing when Liz Brown phoned?

....

3. Why can't Claire go on the picnic?

....

4. Where is the picnic going to be?

....

5. What time will Liz Brown and Mary meet for the picnic?

....

6. What is Mary going to take to the picnic?

....

7. How will they travel to the picnic?

....

Task 2

(Total 14 marks)

THAT IS THE END OF THE LISTENING TASKS. NOW GO ON TO TASK THREE.

3.   **Task Three: At the Picnic (15 marks)**

At the picnic Mark asks Ben some questions. What are his questions? Write them in the spaces. The first one is an example.

Mark: (example) *Do you want a drink, Ben?*

Ben: No thanks. I've already got a bottle of water.

Mark: .... ?

Ben: Yes, I have. We had a picnic here last year.

Mark: .... ?

Ben: We had lots of cake and sandwiches.

Mark: .... ?

Ben: If it rains, we'll run to the car.

Mark: .... ?

Ben: The football match? Yes if I get home in time, I'll watch it.

Mark: .... ?

Ben: No, I'd rather go cycling tomorrow. I can't swim.

Task 3

(Total 15 marks)

Leave blank

4. **Task Four: The Day of the Picnic (5 marks)**

Look at the pictures of the day of the picnic. Draw a line from the pictures to the correct sentences. The first one is an example.

Be careful. There are two extra sentences.

Oh, dear. You've broken it.

Jack's using the phone.

No, thanks. I've had enough.

Stop putting that in your mouth.
It's dirty.

Stop it! That hurt!

There's a toilet in the café over there.

Do you want some more of this cake?

She wants to talk to you.

Task 4

(Total 5 marks)

5. Task Five: Ben Emails Mark (10 marks)

The next week, Ben writes an email to Mark. Fill in the gaps USING ONE WORD IN EACH GAP. The first one is an example.

Hi Mark,

Did (**example**) ....you.......... enjoy the picnic? It was (**1**) .... better than our last picnic. The weather (**2**) .... great and we didn't get wet!

It's (**3**) .... birthday next week and I'm having a party.

(**4**) .... you like to come? It's (**5**) .... Thursday at seven o'clock. I am (**6**) .... to eat a lot of cake and have fun! Please let me know (**7**) .... you can come.

Can you bring your ball to football tomorrow (**8**) .... I've lost mine?

When I go to town next week I (**9**) .... buy a new one. I hope my dad gets (**10**) .... a football shirt for my birthday.

Ben

(Total 10 marks)

6. **Task Six: Another Picnic (20 marks)**

    Later in the year, the Brown family went on another picnic. Look at the pictures and write the story. You must use all the pictures.

    Write about 75 words.

....

....

....

....

....

....

....

....

....

....

Task 6

(Total 20 marks)

TOTAL FOR PAPER: 80 MARKS

THAT IS THE END OF THE TEST

Breakthrough Spoken test

Instructions for the Oral Examiner

Before conducting the oral test the oral examiner must read the guidance notes inside the current version of the booklet "PTE Young Learners Oral Examination Guide". This booklet will be sent to the test centre by email, three weeks before the date of the written examination. If you have any queries, please contact Language Testing Division of Pearson by emailing pltsupport@pearson.com.

Oral Test

The oral test is a compulsory part of the Pearson Test of English Young Learners. Candidates are examined in groups of five by a trained oral examiner who acts as both interviewer and assessor. At each level the oral test lasts 20 minutes and consists of two 10-minute tasks which focus on the language of the level being tested. The oral accounts for 20 marks.

Stages of the Exam

- The candidates do the board game.
- The candidates take turns picking a card from the pack of topic cards and talking about the topic written on it. After each mini-presentation the other candidates and, if needed, the examiner asks the speaker some questions about the topic.

Task 1: The Board Game

- Required: the board game itself (please cut out the squares from the card provided), dice, five coloured counters.

- Lay out the cards in a circle, a line or S-shape.

- Establish the order of turn taking. (E.g. each candidate rolls the dice and the highest scorer goes first).

- The first candidate rolls the dice and moves the appropriate number of squares. The examiner directs the candidate to address the question to another candidate, referred to by name (e.g. "Ask Fatima"). The candidate then reads out the question and the designated candidate answers it. The square is then turned face down to remove it from the game. The turn passes to the next candidate.

- When moving their counters, candidates should count the squares **in English**.

- Each candidate should respond to at least two questions.

The test is over when each candidate has responded to at least two questions. The game should last no longer than 10 minutes for a group of five candidates.

Task 2: Short Talks

The pack of topic cards is placed face down in the middle of the playing area. The first candidate turns over a card and reads the topic written on it. He or she then speaks about that topic for one minute. At the end of one minute the examiner asks the candidate to stop and invites the other candidates to ask follow-up questions, which the first candidate answers. This continues for one minute (giving the candidate a total turn of two minutes' duration). If the other candidates cannot think of any questions, or if they dry up before the minute is up, the examiner should ask questions. The turn then passes to the next candidate.

Breakthrough cards for board game

How long have you been at your school?

What did you give your mum for her last birthday?

What were you doing at ten o'clock last night?

What will you do tomorrow, if you have a headache?

What are your plans for next weekend?

What good films have you seen this year?

What do you bring with you when you come to school?

What job do you want to do in the future?

What did you do when you got up this morning?

How many times have you flown in a plane?

What did you take with you on your last holiday?

Who has a more interesting job? Your mum or your dad?

How many times have you been to the zoo?

How much money have you spent this week?

Is it better to do homework before or after dinner?

What are you going to do when you get home today?

Where do you go to meet your friends at the weekend?

What would you like to do after this test?

How do you feel when you see your grandparents?

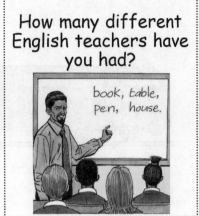

How many different English teachers have you had?

Breakthrough topic cards

A bad day for me and my family

A great day

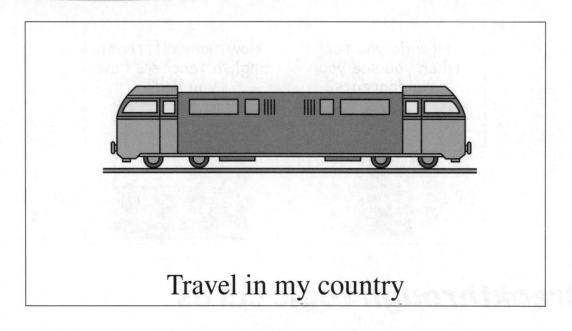

Travel in my country

Transport in my town (city)

A good place to visit in my country

My future job

A fantastic weekend this year

My last holiday

Likes and dislikes at school

My best experience at school

A good experience

A hobby for the future

Friends in my life

My perfect weekend

Pearson Education Limited
KAO Two
KAO Park
Hockham Way,
Harlow, Essex,
CM17 9SR England
and Associated Companies throughout the world.

www.english.com/teamtogether

Original edition © Pearson Italia S.p.A, 2018
This edition © Pearson Education Limited 2020
Published by arrangement with Pearson Italia S.p.A.

First published 2020

ISBN: 978-1-292-29272-4

Set in Bauer Grotesk 12pt

Printed and bound by Golden Cup in China.

Illustrated by Luisa Cittone, Francesca Costa, Adam Linley, Robin Lawrie, Jim Eldridge and Mike Phillips

Cover image: *Front*: **Getty Images:** damircudic